Shadows
on the Beach

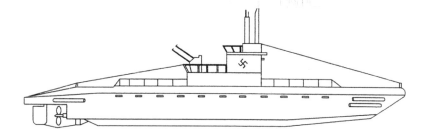

TYPE IXC U-BOAT   Sketch by John T. Maltese

An untold spy story of World War II

by

John T. Maltese

Table of Contents

DEDICATION

It was an adventure into the past to rerun my life and research the incident of that night on the boardwalk in Bradley Beach, NJ where I witnessed the landing of German agents. I was inspired by the Library Of Congress, who was looking for World War II stories as told by the veterans themselves, to write this story so that it may be recorded in history forever.

I dedicate this book to all the courageous American men and woman who fought in World War II and especially to those who gave their lives so that we may live in peace and freedom.

With loving thanks to my wife Virginia and my two sons, Jeffery and John for their assistance and support and many thanks to my brother Jasper Maltese for his help in editing this book.

The Author: John T Maltese

DISCLAIMER

This book is designed to provide personal insight and historical information on an untold spy story of World War II. It is sold or otherwise provided to the public with the understanding that the publisher and author are not attempting to rewrite history. Any individual, organization or institution requiring expert assistance regarding the subject matter in this book should obtain the services of a professional historian.

It is not the purpose of this book to reprint information otherwise available to authors and other creative people, but to complement, amplify and supplement what has already been documented. Readers are encouraged to pursue their interests in matters related to this book to libraries, book stores and the internet. Where resources are abundantly available to anyone interested in the events presented herein.

Historical information was primarily obtained from the material listed in the chapter titled Reference Material.

Every effort has been made to make this book as accurate as possible. However there may be mistakes, both typographical and in content. Therefore the text should be used only as a general guide to the historical event that took place.

An outline of this story has been submitted to the Library of Congress, Washington, DC. Veterans History Project, American Folk life Center. Collection Number AFC/20001/001/2030. No part of this book may be reproduced or transmitted in any form without written permission from the author.

AUTHORS NOTES

The scene, World War II where up to now most books that were written about German U-Boats landing spies on our beaches, were written about spy activities up to 1943. This book will take you into1943 and beyond.

Read About:

- The results of a six year research program into U-Boat/Spy activities.

- The unpublished spy landings as reported by eye witnesses.

- An untold story of a German spy landing that took place on our beaches.

- Why Adolph Hitler endangered one of his U-Boats as well as the crew for a highly secret mission, here in the USA, near the end of the war.

- How Hitler made a last chance effort to win World War II with his new secret weapons and how close he came to using them.

- The secret weapon that Hitler did unleash against the Allies fortunately without success. This one was too little too late.

INTRODUCTION

This is the story of a twelve year old boy, along with his cousin and friends who witnessed the landing of four German agents on the shore at Bradley Beach, New Jersey one warm summer night. Even though he called the Coast Guard Life Saving Station on Shark River Inlet in Avon, NJ at the time of the landing, these agents were never captured. Can you imagine a young boy trying to convince the Coast Guard Officer that four German agents just landed on the beach? Finally convinced, he agreed to investigate. By the time the military arrived the agents had plenty of time to change their clothes, walk up on the boardwalk and blend in with the people strolling on the ocean front walkway.

Now on the boardwalk they walked into the future, never to be heard from again. Where did they go and who met them to show them the way? What were they doing here in the USA, what was their mission? They had a specific mission that's described in this book as Adolph Hitler's last attempt to win the war with his new secret weapons. Read about the U-Boat that was in the right place at the right time to make the Bradley Beach, NJ landing.

Now in my late 70's the memory of that landing has been entrenched in my mind for years. I now feel the need to offer my contribution to World War II History by writing this story "Shadows on the Beach".

December 8, 1941 Adolph Hitler declares war on the United States of America just one day after the Imperial Japanese Empire bombed Pearl Harbor. One of his schemes was to infiltrate the American Industrial War Machine with spies, saboteurs and special agents to disrupt our manufacturing process of war material.

With many German sympathizers already living in America and ready to defend the Fatherland, a plan of action was established.

The plan established was to deliver spies, saboteurs and special agents to the shores of America. Adolph Hitler in conjunction with Admiral Karl Doenitz, who then was the Grand Commander of all German U-Boats, decided to deliver these German agents to our shores using Doenitz's U-Boat. The Admiral did not want to risk his U-Boats to make these deliveries since the early years of the war his U-Boats were sinking Allied ships faster than we were building them.

In any case, Adolph Hitler insisted that U-Boats be used to make the drop-offs. These agents were very well trained at Lake Quenz School near Berlin. The school taught espionage activities. They were well equipped with explosives, detonators, money, clothing, etc.

The primary mission of these agents was to disrupt the "American Industrial War Machine" in order to slow down the mighty production process of the United States by blowing up power stations, bridges, railroads and more. Between 1942 & 1945 there were several landings on the American coast. The most notable were the landings on Long Island, New York and

Jacksonville, FL in mid 1942.

These are the landings that we know about because all these agents either gave themselves up or were outright captured. Two agents from the New York group turned themselves in to the FBI. They told the FBI where to find the rest of their group in New York and the group in Jacksonville, FL.

By strict orders given by J. Edgar Hoover, then the Director of the FBI, enemy agents, whether they were captured or surrendered, were to be promptly turned over to the FBI for interrogation. They gave secret information to the FBI such as the number of men in their party, the purpose of their mission, what targets they were to attack and the U-Boat that brought them here.

But what about the landing where agents were not captured and the only record was a group of eye witnesses, people who happen to be in the area when the landing took place.

Some eye witnesses telephoned the authorities and informed them of their find only to have that call declared a "hoax" or the reply was "we cannot talk about enemy activity" No action was taken.

This book puts together a puzzle that depicts the events of that summer night in Bradley Beach when the enemy landed on our shores.

John T Maltese

CHAPTER ONE

THE BUNGALOW

Bradley Beach, New Jersey, a summer resort town on the Atlantic Ocean about sixty miles south of New York City. A very popular resort town for people from Northern New Jersey, New York City and even the Philadelphia, PA area. The town was incorporated in 1893 and founded by James A Bradley, who owned lots of property in the area.

The town has single family bungalows, rooming houses, bed and breakfast lodging and hotels. It's a true resort town with a variety of accommodations, restaurants and entertainment. A beach front boardwalk for ocean view strolling, extends from Asbury Park and Ocean Grove, NJ in the north and to Avon, NJ. in the south.

Avon, NJ is the location of the Coast Guard Station on the Shark River Inlet. The railroad provided transportation from northern New Jersey and New York City directly to the Bradley Beach train station. There was also a double decker bus, operated by Coast City Coaches, that ran between Belmar, NJ to Asbury Park, NJ making stops in Avon and Bradley Beach.

Asbury Park was an entertainment city on the beach, which was very popular for its rides for both kids and adults. A Ferris Wheel, merry go round, and two convention halls on the boardwalk that provided live entertainment with dancing. I remember sneaking into the Convention Hall on the boardwalk to see Harry James and his orchestra, including his wife Betty Grable. There were a number of elaborate movie houses owned by the Reed Organization.

The Organization also owned and operated the Monte Carlo swimming pool located on the boardwalk with walking access to the beach in Asbury Park. People from surrounding towns would drive, walk or take the bus to spend a day in Asbury Park. The amusement town provided activity for all surrounding resort communities.

Bradley Beach was then and still is a popular resort town on the Jersey Shore. Today I feel fortunate to have spent my summers, as a youth, in Bradley Beach. Even when I was bringing up my own kids we continued to go to Bradley Beach and they followed in my footsteps with the good times on the beach and boardwalk. Lets not forget the trips to Asbury Park.

My parents rented in Bradley Beach for the summer months since 1939 staying in rooming houses, such as the McAlear house on Newark Ave and the Mount house on Ocean Park Ave. They also rented a bungalow on Newark Ave. Newark Ave was like Main St. USA with food shopping, candy store, vegetable market, and a fish market with fresh fish brought in by Wooleys Boats whose large boats were docked right on the beach.

The boats were placed on rollers and pulled up on the beach by a bull dozer. They sold fish right from their boats before delivering the fresh fish to the market on Newark Ave. Many times I went with my mom to the beach just to buy fish.

The hurricane of 1947 destroyed the boardwalk, took Wooley's boats off the beach and over the damaged boardwalk and ocean front road and carried them into Fletcher's Lake. At that north end of the beach, there was the Atlantic Ocean, the boardwalk and then came the Lake. With the boardwalk gone the heavy winds caused a tidal surge that floated the boats right into the lake.

Then came an opportunity for my family to buy a bungalow on Ocean Park Ave on the corner of Central Ave. My father and his two brothers, immigrant shoe repair men by trade, pooled their resources together and bought it. Now the family had a home to go to in the summer. Their own place right in Bradley Beach and only two blocks from the beach. It had three bedrooms on the first floor with knotty pine panels on the walls and ceilings for the Aunts and Uncles, a small kitchen, a dinning area and one bathroom all on the first floor.

It also had three separate sleeping areas in an unfinished attic for their twelve kids. Separated by a long curtain where the boy cousins slept and front room where the girl cousins slept. As I look back at it, it was a small house for so many relatives. But at the time it was a huge house for all to enjoy and escape the summer heat.

My father's family had six people, my uncle Jasper had six people and my uncle Tony had five for a total of seventeen of us. This is before my fathers third brother, uncle Pete and family of three returned after serving in the Navy during World War II. When my uncle Pete did get back we needed more room. The dinning room was converted to a fourth bedroom.

The house was raised to dig out a new basement and then lowered and we finished the basement with knotty pine walls, block ceiling and painted the concrete floor. The whole basement was a big kitchen with four family size tables, two refrigerators, two stoves for cooking and a large sink. Each family had a cabinet used as a food pantry.

Yes, we were twenty in all. Fortunately my father and my three uncles were only at the bungalow on weekends, that is Saturday night and all day Sunday.

Depending on traffic they would return to the city either Sunday night or early Monday morning, where they had three shoe repair shops. It did get quite interesting sometimes when I think back especially during meal times and not to mention the one bathroom and an outdoor cold shower. Our parents were glad when us kids went to the beach after breakfast and didn't come back until dinner time. When our parents came to the beach they brought us our lunch.

They brought our lunch so we had no need to go back to the bungalow. They had everything all figured out for us. After dinner us cousins all went to roam on the boardwalk for several hours. Everyday was a beach day except when it rained and then we went to the movies in Asbury Park or cleaned our fishing reels. I remember those rainy days. The rain always managed to disrupt our daily schedule. I remember on occasion we would go to the beach in the rain with only our beach umbrellas. The umbrellas would keep us dry. All in all we had some very busy summers at the beach when we were kids.

But when it rained, we did get one dollar each from our parents and that was after an hour of begging and pleading. Then we were off to Asbury Park where we paid .75 cents for the movie and .25 cents for a drink at the Soda mat on the boardwalk.

I recall a discussion during breakfast one Sunday morning, where the grown ups were talking about an unusual incident that took place on the beach on the previous night, which some of us cousins knew about.

I also remember another discussion taking place at the dinning room table as we kids were making our way out to go to the beach. This was a significant recall since now I needed to determine the date that this incident happened. I know we were living in the bungalow at the time and it was a weekend because our dads were with us.

The unusual activity took place on a Saturday night and our parents were having a discussion that following Sunday morning. Remembering that discussion, I needed to find out what year the bungalow was purchased. This would verify the year the incident took place.

Pictured here is our Bungalow located on
219 Ocean Park Ave, Bradley Beach, NJ.

Photo taken by the author's family

CHAPTER TWO

THE BEGINNING

In the beginning it must be noted that the reason for writing this book is a result of a magazine article I read in my Chiropractor's waiting room some time around July, 2002. I don't remember the name of the magazine but the article was very explicit that American veterans should document their World War II stories as given by those who lived it and experienced the horrors of war.

Over the years there are thousands of untold war stories that have not been told by Veterans. War experiences that they never talked about, these stories are priceless. If these stories are not gathered now they will soon disappear into history and never be told.

A program to document these experiences would bring a new thrust to Washington, DC. The Library of Congress is sponsoring a new project called "Veterans History Project" whereby volunteers, Veterans families or the Veteran can interview veterans so their experiences may be documented.

The objective is to get the real truth by letting our Veterans tell their stories and write them down, documenting them with pictures and letters. Then get them over to the "Veterans History Project" c/o The Library of Congress in Washington, DC. You can find a complete address on the last page of this chapter.

By documenting these experiences it would give future generations a collection of monumental wealth in oral histories, written material, pages of diaries, letters and photos that have never been seen before. These stories that have never been told, would be of great value for future generations.

Reading this article brought me to the memories of my own family members who served in the military. I knew they had real stories to tell, although they rarely talked about their experiences of the war. I knew a little bit of what they did.

My Cousin Carmine Pinto was a marine in the South Pacific. During one battle on a South Pacific Island his unit was being driven back into the sea by a strong enemy. Running for his life towards the sea, he picked up a dead body and pulled the body over his back for protection from enemy bullets. As he went in to the water he started to swim as fast as he could. He later woke up on Naval Hospital Ship not ever knowing how he got there. He later found out there was a detail of Marines, with small boats, who were assigned to pick up dead and wounded bodies floating in the water. It was a miracle he survived.

My cousin Carmine did survive the war.

My Uncle Sal Cirinese was on constant alert during the Battle of the Bulge and was wounded three times during the long siege at the city of Bastogne. After his wounds were repaired he was back on the front line.

The third time he walked around for two days with a bullet in his back before he passed out. The medics carried him back to the field hospital. They were low on food, ammunition and supplies. They also had to fight another enemy and that was the bad weather, the cold and it seemed that the winter snow was endless. It was hard to get around in the deep snow but it did give the GI's good cover from the enemy.

He told me it was heaven when the snow stopped and the new supplies and ammunition were parachuted in to their position. The low flying C47 Cargo planes were dropping everything from food, to medical supplies, ammunition and lots more including some mail from home to pick-up the morale of the fighting men. That day was a grand finale of the Battle of the Bulge.

My uncle Sal did survive the war.

My Uncle Peter Maltese served on an LST in the South Pacific. He took part in several island invasions, especially the invasion of the Philippines. Knowing my uncle as a real low key gentleman type person whose love was to cook big meals.

I don't know how he got his battle station as the stern anti-aircraft gun. During one invasion they were being attacked by Japanese Zeros.

At that battle he did manage to shoot down a Zero, much to his surprise. He recalled the burning Zero came right over his gun station taking one of the ships radio antennas with him. The pilot of the plane was probably trying to take out my uncle and his gun station but he failed to do so. The Zero crashed and exploded and my Uncle went on to live another day.

As I said he loved to cook before, during and after the war. When he made tomato sauce on board ship for spaghetti, the crew, including the captain, used to stand in line to get a cup full of sauce just to drink it. It was that good. These boys on board his LST had a tough time fighting in the South Pacific but I can assure you they ate well.

My uncle Pete did survive the war.

My brother-in-law John Handago served in the European campaign with the 63rd Infantry Division and fought in the battle of Southern France and Germany just after D-Day June 6, 1944.

At this battle, resistance from the enemy was light since Hitler had concentrated most all of his fighting forces to the D-Day invasion. Therefore the Allies encountered fewer casualties in this area.

This allowed him and his buddies to relax and sit on the curb side for that moment. They were hungry and didn't have any money to buy a cup of coffee and donuts, which was available. Only the few guys who had a couple of bucks in their pockets were able to buy coffee and donuts.

My brother-in-law John did survive the war.

My uncle John Maltese was stationed on a Navy tanker in the South Pacific. His ship supplied fuel to lots of fighting ships. One day as his tanker was returning from a mission they were assigned to dock in position 24 along side one of the South Pacific Islands. When his ship arrived on the scene, by mistake the position was occupied by another ship, so his tanker was redirected and ordered to dock in position 30. That night, during a bombing raid, Japanese airplanes sunk the ship docked in position 24, there was a massive explosion.

The ship docked in position 24, sank in minutes and all hands were lost. A stroke of good luck for my uncle. Bad luck for his shipmates on the other ship.

My uncle John did survive the war.

I could not pass on mentioning my father-in-law, Paul Cardiello, who fought in the "War to end all Wars", World War I. He was a member of 114th Infantry Division with a rank of Corporal which was part of the New Jersey National Guard formed at Camp McClellan, Alabama in July 1917. They landed in France in July 1918 and assigned to the Alsace region. There they would be trained in raiding enemy lines north of Verdun as part of Meuse-Argonne offensive. They were engaged in battle with the enemy thru September 1918. During active combat his unit captured 2,187 German prisoners and 6,159 men killed, wounded or missing in action.

Paul Cardiello was a World War I hero who fought across France and was wounded in the "Battle of Verdun" As he was crossing a wooden bridge with his men, a German sniper fires his gun and got him in the right thigh.

He received the Purple Heart for his wounds and a medal from the French government for his bravery fighting across France. He was a real American proud to be out there defending his beloved country and fighting to preserve our liberty and freedom.

Above is a plaque with his medals, ribbons and Purple Heart

When he returned home to Garfield, NJ, he became a member of the Garfield Veterans of Foreign Wars and served as president of the VFW for two terms.

He helped build the original VFW club house in Garfield along with his buddies, who were also members of the VFW. He was also a volunteer of the Garfield Fire Company # 2 for many years. During a great fire at Hayden Chemical Co. in Garfield, NJ, Paul stood on top of a high chemical tank full of explosive material. With a water hose, he kept the tank wet to keep it cool so it would not explode. As he did in World War I he put his own life on the line to protect others.

He was also a Boy Scout Master and for many years took his Scout Troop out camping all over the surrounding area of Bergen County, New Jersey.

Last but not least this is the military career of the author John T. Maltese. When the Korean War broke out in June 1950 I was assigned to the 50th Armored Division, National Guard Unit in Jersey City, NJ.

I was married in 1952 and deferred from the draft until 1953. Towards the end of the Korean conflict I was then drafted into the regular Army and was ordered to report to Camp Kilmer, NJ. From Camp Kilmer I received orders to report to Fort Chaffee, Arkansas for basic training in field artillery.

The basic training consisted of two months of Infantry training and two months of artillery training specializing in communications. Running telephone wire from the Gun positions to the OP, observation post. Upon completion of basic training we were going to be shipped to the State of Washington to board a troop ship bound for Korea. After drawing all my winter gear for Korea and on the last day of my training I was ordered to report to the Commanding Officer as they sent a Jeep to pick me up in the field.

My commanding officer told me I had ten minutes to pack my duffle bag because I had to board a train in Little Rock, AK bound for Camp Kilmer, NJ. Here I would get a two week leave so I could be with my family over the Christmas and New Year holidays.

Then reporting back to Camp Kilmer, I received orders to proceed to board a troop ship in Bayonne, NJ for shipment to Livorno, Italy. From Livorno I would report to Camp Roeder, Salzburg, Austria. This trip over the Atlantic Ocean took fifteen cold, stormy days. It was my worst boating trip ever. I was in the North Atlantic in a January storm that buried the bow of my ship in water every minute.

Upon arriving in Salzburg I was assigned to the 510 th Field Artillery Battalion where I assumed a position of communication lineman. My rank at that time was corporal. My battalion was part of the United States Forces Austria as part of the Liberation of Austria from the Germans. There was the British Army, the Russian Army and the US Army each took an equal part of the country.

I spent the next eighteen months doing military exercises; we occasionally had a combined maneuver with the

British. We would spend two weeks in Grafenvor, Germany doing simulated battle. More training, I spent four months in Military school in Linz, Austria. The same school where Germany trained their SS troopers. Then there were the Alerts.

Alerts would be called without any warning whereby we would have to pack our things and board the two and half ton trucks. My group had two of its own three quarter ton trucks. When all was ready we formed a convoy and headed for our Gun Position in eastern Austria. Once when the Russians moved several divisions towards the Linz River, our commanders called a red alert meaning this was real.

After setting up the 105 Howitzers we were on standby for battle for the next two days. When the Russians turned away from the Linz River, the alert was called off. The Russians claimed they were only on a training maneuver. It sure scared the hell out of us.

I was on my way home in June, 1955. I had my duffel bag packed ready for transportation to the train station in Salzburg where I boarded a train bound for Italy. I boarded a troop ship in Livorno, Italy. While cruising in the Mediterranean Sea towards the Gibraltar ship sprung a leak in the one of the propeller shafts and we had to stop in Casablanca for two days to get it repaired. Finally underway and in the middle of the Atlantic we got a distress call from an American freighter.

The freighter was named the "American Cotton" one of the crew members needed surgery for appendicitis. Our ship sitting dead in the water, we sent a boat to pick up the patient. Our ship had a full hospital on board and the surgery took all day.

Again we were underway, thank God, as we were all very anxious to get home. Fifteen days after leaving Livorno, Italy we arrived in New York with the Statue of Liberty welcoming us back. A feeling that was beyond words.

I was glad to be home to see my wife and a brand new son that I had not met yet. I was discharged from Fort Dix, NJ. Now that my military career was finished, I needed to get back to civilian life.

* * * * * * * * * *

After contacting Washington, DC, I did get some applications from the Library of Congress History Project for my family members. They could now document their war stories and file them with the "Veterans History Project". I encouraged my family to interview the veteran in the family so their stories could be recorded forever.

Then one day it hit me! I had my own story about a spy landing in Bradley Beach, NJ. This could be my contribution to the Veterans History Project, it could turn out to be my contribution to World War II.

To complete my story, I began a massive research program that would last over six years. I was an eyewitness, along with my cousin and a couple of friends, to a German U-boat landing four spies on the beach. The image of these men landing on the rock jetty, then coming on shore and on to the under side of the boardwalk pavilion was scary.

That was in the back of my mind for many, many years, it was almost forgotten. Yet it was always there on my mind and I always wanted to document the story. Time passes pretty fast when you get married and start bringing up a family.

I was only a young boy at the time, just twelve and a half years old. I am now seventy seven and the magazine article I found in the Chiropractors office really encouraged me to submit my story to the *Library of Congress, Veterans History Project.*

The magazine article had rekindled the story and transported me back in history to World War II and my youth in Bradley Beach, NJ.

Yes, I did submit the story to the Library of Congress and received a letter from the Director of the project. A copy of the letter is at the end of this Chapter.

I received a letter from Ellen McCulloch-Lovell, Director of the "Veterans History Project" and she told me it was a great story. She also requested a picture of me taken at the time of the incident. After searching my files I did manage to find one and she filed it with my story.

She did say there is one thing missing. A very important piece of information that would complete the story and that is the month and the year the landing took place. Later in my life it became a big problem because all I could remember was it took place in the summer months.

I didn't know what year it was. It would have been 1942, 1943, or 1944? The directors request was not easy, it sent me into a research project that will last six years. I had to do lots of reading, lots of visits to libraries and National Archives including the Archives Museum in Germany.

It quickly became evident that this project was turning out to be a monstrous puzzle and it was a matter of putting all the pieces together.

VETERANS
HISTORY
PROJECT

September 23, 2002

Dear Mr. Maltese:

Thank you for participating in the Veterans History Project as a member of the Volunteer Corps. The Library of Congress and its American Folklife Center gratefully acknowledge the receipt of the documentary materials that chronicle your wartime memories.

Your participation in this historic and important project will contribute to the development of a lasting body of knowledge chronicling the wartime memories and experience of the nations' war veterans. Future generations will be grateful to be able to learn from those who served. The collection of recorded oral histories, written material, papers, diaries, letters and photographs will be of untold value to scholars, students, and veterans' descendants in the decades ahead.

Thank you for supporting and becoming a part of the Veterans History Project.

Sincerely,

Ellen McCulloch-Lovell
Director of the Veterans History Project

Veterans History Project
American Folklife Center
Library of Congress
101 Independence Ave., SE
Washington, DC 20540-4615

tel: 202-707-4916
msg: 1-888-371-5848
fax: 202-252-2046
email: vohp@loc.gov
www.loc.gov/folklife/vets

Mr. John T. Maltese
2111 SW 15th Place
Deerfield Beach, FL 33442

John Maltese Collection: Veterans History Project (American Folklife Center, Library of Congress)   Page 1 of 1

The Library of Congress >> American Folklife Center

ABOUT
SEARCH/BROWSE
HELP
COPYRIGHT

Home » Search Results » **Full Description**

John Maltese Collection

Biographical Information

Name:
John T. Maltese
Date of Birth:
1932
Place of Birth:
Ridgefield Park, NJ

Gender:
Male
Race:
Unspecified
Home State:
FL
War or Conflict:
Korean War, 1950-1955
Status:
Civilian
Prisoner of War:
Unknown
Service Related Injury:
Unknown
Service History Note:
Maltese is a veteran of the Korean war, but collection
consists of story of when he was younger. In 1944,
Maltese and his cousin observed spy activity and turned
them into the authorities.

Collection Information

Type of Resource:
Manuscript: Memoirs [1 item] --Typewritten document
Photograph: Copy photographic print [1 item] --Portrait
Donor:
John T. Maltese
Collection #:
AFC/2001/001/2030
Subjects:
Maltese, John
Korean War, 1950-1955 -- Personal Narratives
Cite as:
John Maltese Collection (AFC/2001/001/2030), Veterans
History Project, American Folklife Center, Library of
Congress

Home » Search Results » **Full Description**

CHAPTER THREE

THE U-BOAT WARS

My research brought me to the U-boat wars of 1942. Visiting the local newspaper and library I found that U-Boats were sinking Allied ships right off the coast of America. One of the perils of war that frightened Prime Minister Winston Churchill was the number of U-Boats in the Atlantic. They were sinking his war material that England needed so desperately. The U-Boats gathered in what was called "Wolf Packs" and they would attack in a group that made it easier to sink a specific target.

They infiltrated up and down the coast of the USA and even into the Caribbean and towards the Gulf of Mexico.

Besides torpedoing Allied ships they were also known to lay mine fields in strategic areas such as entrances to our seaports and shipping lanes.

Fortunately the Allies were able to break the German Radio Code or the Enigma machine by capturing a U-Boat or weather ship with the Enigma in tack. Allies were able decode their messages and redirected the convoys to avoid any contact with U-Boats.

Another problem for Germany was that some torpedoes were on our side when they failed to detonate, ran at a lower depth or even ran astray. Later on in the war Germany developed a torpedo that would run straight and then when it detected a loud noise, such as the ships engines, it turned to that target and detonated. Unfortunately these torpedoes had their problems with the steering mechanism which was not reliable.

Towards the end of the war U-Boats were fitted with a Schnorchel that allowed the sub to breath while under water. It supplied air to the diesel engines as well the batteries being charged while the sub was submerged.

This gave the U-Boat an advantage that it could lay under water, undetected, until an Allied ship arrived on the scene. German U-Boats were also used to drop off spies, saboteurs and special agents to set up observation/weather stations along our coast.

At the National Achieves they found that German subs patrolled from Maine to Florida to New Orleans. There was information that indicated there had been German spy landings during this time. These landings were very well documented because the spies who were captured or surrendered to the FBI told all about their mission.

During my research to find some link to the "Bradley Beach Landing" I found lots of other information about war time news and a spy landing. A spy landing that took place on Long Island, New York on June 13, 1942. On that day, in the early morning hours, a German U-Boat Kapitan brought his boat into the foggy coast of Amagansett, Long Island, NY. His mission was to land four German saboteurs on Amagansett.

These very well trained German agents came ashore and brought four wooden crates with them.

These crates contained explosives, clothes, cash dollars, detonators etc. Their purpose was to sabotage the Hellsgate Bridge in NY, the Pennsylvania Railroad Depot in Newark, NJ, power plants, attack the main water pipes of New York City and other war time targets of opportunity.

The German Submarine U-202 under the command of Kapitanleutnant Hans-Heinz Linder crossed the Atlantic to make the drop off on the beaches of Long Island. Linder Intentionally brought his boat up on a sandbar until the spies were underway in their rubber boat. Unfortunately he ran his boat onto the sandbar during an outgoing tide, which was a terrible mistake on the part of the Kapitan, it left his boat helpless on the beach.

The four spies rowed their inflatable toward the shore and made it to the beach. The U-202 was still struggling to get off the sandbar while the spies had already changed their cloths, buried their crates and were on their way to New York City. Linder realized that daylight was coming real soon and he was far up a ground and was getting things ready to scuttle his boat and surrender his crew.

The Kapitan and his crew would have given themselves up to the Coast Guard and they would have become prisoners of war, when he finally broke free of the sandbar. Even though the U-Boat was spotted by civilians on the beach, their cry for help was ignored when the Coast Guard Station on the beach called it a false report. As the tide was rising the U-202 managed to escape and made it out to sea.

Almost a year later the U-202 was sunk on June, 1943, 18 dead, 30 survivors. On June 17, 1942 a similar landing took place where four other saboteurs were dropped off at Ponte Verde Beach, Florida near Jacksonville by U-584 under the command of Kapitanleutnant Joachim Deecke.

Their purpose was the same as the NY group, to perform sabotage activity here in the USA. Both the New York landing and the Florida landing were part of "Operation Pastorius". U-584 was sunk in October 1943; all hands were lost.

Fortunately for the United States two German spies from the New York group gave themselves up to the FBI.

When they gave themselves up to the FBI they gave the names and location of the other six. As a result all eight espionage agents were captured and six were executed as German spies, except the two who surrendered themselves to the FBI. They were given prison sentences and after the war President Truman pardoned both German agents and they were deported back to Germany.

It's time to note that the Director of the FBI, J. Edgar Hoover issued strict orders that captured spies were to be turned over to the FBI for interrogation. Their capture was to be kept top secret and information was not to be shared with anyone.

These landings were kept secret from the public until the FBI arrived on the scene. The identity of these spies was kept secret until the FBI had released the information to the public.

As a matter of interest while doing research at the National Archives and Record Administration in College Park, Md., I was told that there were eyewitnesses to a landing at Outer Banks, NC.

This was reported by the Raleigh Newspaper. Here there were also eyewitnesses, but since no one was ever caught, the incident was never officially documented. By order of J. Edgar Hoover the incident was never released to the general public for fear of creating a panic that the enemy had landed on our shores.

Another fascinating story that I came upon while re-searching, was a story that appeared in the Palm Beach, FL Sun-Sentinel Newspaper on October 21, 2005. More than 60 years ago in June 1942, spies from a German U-Boat landed on the beach in Boca Raton, FL and occupied a beach front home. The house stood empty all year except when the owners lived there for a few months in winter. The home had a large window overlooking the Atlantic Ocean.

At that window site was a large telescope and a signaling device used to signal U-Boats regarding Allied ships off the coast of Florida. As a result, there were 16 Allied ships sunk off the shore of Boca Raton, FL. Today, there is a plaque on the site, which is dedicated to all the Veterans of World War II.

These spies were never caught and again by the order of J. Edgar Hoover this incident was never released to the general public, therefore there isn't any official record of this incident, but there were eyewitnesses.

Besides German spy landings on our coast there were many U-Boats operating off the coast of New Jersey / New York. Following is a list of U-Boats, some of their accomplishments against the Allies and their fate between 1942 and 1944. These U-Boats did a tremendous amount of damage to the Allied war effort. Tons of military equipment went to the bottom of the Atlantic Ocean. All this damage took place just off the Jersey shore and just outside the port of New York.

- **U-71:** Under the command of Kapitanleutnant Walte Flachsenberg, operated off the New York/New Jersey coast. On March 17, 1942 torpedoed and sank the tanker MV Ranga. March 20, 1942 torpedoed and sank the SS Oakmar. March 26, 1942 torpedoed and sank the SS Dixie Arrow. March 31, 1942 torpedoed and sank the SS San Gerado.
  Fate: U-Boat scuttled on May 2, 1945.

- **U-84:** Under the command of Kapitanleutnant Horst Uphoff had orders to patrol between New York Harbor and Cape Hatteras. No contact with Allied ships

  Fate: U-Boat sunk August 24, 1943, all hands lost.

- **U-103:** Under the command of Kapitanleutnant Werner Winter, operated off the New Jersey/ New York

coast. On February 5, 1942 torpedoed and sank the
tanker SS India Arrow and the SS China Arrow.
Fate: U-Boat scuttled on May 3, 1945

- **U-106:** Under the command of Kapitanleutnant
Herman Rasch, operated off the coast of New Jersey/
New York. On January 3,1942 torpedoed and sank the
SS EmpireWildebeete.
Fate: U-Boat sunk August 2, 1943; survivors were the
Commander and 35 men. 25 hands were lost.

- **U-130:** Under the command of Korvkpt Ernst Kals
operating off the coast of Atlantic City, NJ. Torpedoed
and sank the tanker MV Alexander Hoegh on December
12, 1941. Also sank the MV Varanger on December 25,
1941.
Fate: U-Boat sunk March 13, 1943. All hands lost.

- **U-135:** Under the command of Kapitanleutnant
Friedrich Hermann Praetorius. On May 17, 1942
torpedoed and sank the SS Fort Quapplle east of New
Jersey/New York Harbor.
Fate: U-Boat sunk on July 15, 1943. Commander
along with 41 of his crew survived. 5 hands lost.

- **U-136:** Under the command of Kapitanleutnant
Heinrich Zimmermann. Torpedoed and sank the SS
Arundo on March 28,1942 just south of New York
Harbor.
Fate: U-Boat sunk July 11, 1942. All hands lost.

- **U-202:** Under the command of Kapitanleutnant Hans
  – Heinz Linder, boat landed four saboteurs on
  Amagansett, Long Island, New York on June 27, 1942.
  All four saboteurs were captured. On June 22, 1942
  torpedoed and sank the SS Rio Tercero east of the New
  Jersey/ New York coast.
  Fate: U-Boat sunk June 2, 1943. The Commander and
  27 of his crew were rescued. 18 hands lost

- **U-373:** Under the command of Kapitanleutnant Paul
  Karl Loeser. On March 22, 1942 torpedoed and sank the
  MV Thursobank SE off New Jersey/New York coast.
  Fate: U-Boat was sunk June 8, 1944. Commander
  along with 46 of his crew survived. 4 hands lost.

- **U-432:** Under the command of Kapitanleutnant Heize-
  Otto Schultze. Patrolling east of New Jersey/New York on
  May 23, 1942 she torpedoed and sank the SS
  Zurichmoor.
  Fate: U-Boat was sunk March 11, 1943. Commander
  along with 26 of his crew were lost. 20 survived as
  POW's.

- **U-578:** Under the command of Korvettkapitan Ernst
  – August Rehwinkel. While on patrol southeast of New
  Jersey/New York torpedoed and sank the MV
  Polyphemus on May 27, 1942 and torpedoed and sank
  the MV Berenganger on June 2, 1942.
  Fate: U-Boat was sunk August 10, 1942. All hands lost.

- **U-593:** Under the command of Kapitanleutnant
  Gerd Kelbing. While patrolling East/Northeast of
  Atlantic City she torpedoed and damaged the SS Stavras
  on May 14, 1942. Also on May 25, 1942 torpedoed and
  sank the tanker MV Persephone east of Barnegat Light,
  New Jersey.
  Fate: U-Boat was Scuttled December 12, 1943. Entire
  crew survived.

- **U-571:** Under the command of Kapitanleutnant
  Helmut Mohlmann. While patrolling east of New Jersey/
  New York torpedoed and sank the SS Hertford on
  March 29, 1942.
  Fate: U-Boat was sunk January 28, 1944, All hands lost.

- **U-869:** Under the command of Kapitanleutnant
  Hellmut Neuerburg, after its training and shake down
  cruise in March 1944 she was ordered to patrol the New
  Jersey coast, south of New York City in May 1944.
  In December, 1944.she was ordered on a second patrol
  to the New Jersey coast.
  Fate: Up to the end of World War II the fate and the
  location of the U-869 was unknown.

Admiral Karl Doenitz, Commander in Chief of the
German submarine Navy, "Kreigsmarine" told Adolph Hitler that
he refused to endanger his U-boats by dropping off spies on
beaches of America only for them to be captured.

The June 1942 landings had accounted for eight saboteurs to be captured, four in New York, and four in Florida.

In 1942 during the Battle of the Atlantic U-boats were sinking Allied ships everyday. Doenitz wanted his boats to continue to sink Allied ships instead of dropping off spies and running a shuttle service for Adolph Hitler.

This pause of spy drop-offs proved that the year 1942 was not the year of the Bradley Beach landing. Admiral Doenitz defied Hitler and did not use his U-boats for this purpose for the remainder of 1942. That leaves 1943 or 1944 as the Bradley Beach drop off years.

THE U-BOAT WARS

Wall tied to WWII incident

Boca Raton plans dedication Nov. 12

BY MARY THURMAN YUHAS
SPECIAL CORRESPONDENT

For more than 60 years, the 6-foot Sanborn wall that runs along the sidewalk from State Road A1A between the Beresford and The Excelsior condominiums to the beach has stood as a silent witness to events that took place during World War II.

But recent information has shed light on its historical significance, and on Nov. 12 the wall will be commemorated. Boca Raton Mayor Steven Abrams will unveil a 12-by-18-inch cast bronze plaque, according to Emily Lilly, the city's community affairs and resource specialist.

The plaque reads: "On this spot in June 1942, spies from German U-boats landed and occupied Dr. William Sanborn's home, built on this site in 1937. The subs, deployed during World War II as part of Hitler's Operation Drumbeat, torpedoed tankers and freighters traveling the East Coast shipping lane, carrying vital supplies to the U.S. and England. The Germans sank 397 ships and killed 5,000 people. Twenty-four ships sank off the coast of Florida, 16 between Cape Canaveral and Boca Raton."

IF YOU GO

What: Dedication of historical World War II Sanborn wall.

When: 9 a.m. Nov. 12.

Where: Sanborn wall runs along public sidewalk access to the ocean between The Excelsior and Beresford condominiums at 350 S. Ocean Blvd. in Boca Raton. Refreshments following in South Pavilion, East Palmetto Park Road and State Road A1A.

Cost: Free

Parking: South Beach Pavilion or south end of South Beach Park, 400 N. State Road A1A. Trolley available for people unable to walk ¼-quarter mile to dedication site.

Contact: Emily Lilly, community affairs and resource specialist for city of Boca Raton, 561-393-7827.

Both the city and the Boca Raton Army Air Field Preservation Society planned the dedication, which is part of Boca Raton's, "Salute to Veterans," for Veterans Day, Nov. 11, Lilly said.

The society is a group of citizens recently formed to preserve some of the buildings from the field that are still standing on what is now Florida Atlantic University's Boca Raton campus, according to Susan Gillis, archivist for the Boca Raton Historical Society in Boca Raton.

The field was 5,820 acres and extended from Dixie Highway to the Seaboard Railroad and from Spanish River Road to Palmetto Park Road. It is estimated that close to 100,000 troops transitioned through there from 1942 through '47, according to Gillis.

Speakers at the dedication will include Dr. Peter Barrett, 71, of Rancho Palos Verdes, Calif., who lived next door to the Sanborn house during the war, and William Sanborn Hutchins of North Palm Beach, Sanborn's great nephew.

WALL CONTINUES ON 6

THE U-BOAT WARS

SUN-SENTINEL NEWS
6 FRIDAY, OCTOBER 21, 2005 ·

HISTORICAL IMPACT: The Nov. 12 dedication of the Sanborn wall will be part of a 'Salute to Veterans' celebration organized by Boca Raton. **Photo courtesy of Boca Raton Recreation Services**

Boca Raton to dedicate Sanborn wall

■ WALL

CONTINUED FROM PAGE 1

In June 1942, around 2 a.m. one morning, Barrett's mother, Jessie, heard loud knocking at their front door, Peter Barrett said. His father, Hollis, was in Chicago working on the war effort.

When his mother answered, two military men told her that a distant neighbor had seen flashing lights signaling from their house. Barrett, then 7, looked harder into the darkness. "I realized half a dozen soldiers with guns and combat gear were standing there," he said.

During the war, Barrett said windows had to be completely covered at night to prevent any light from escaping that could aid the enemy.

Barrett's mother assured the men that the signaling was not coming from their house, but told them that the house next door, the Sanborns', stood empty most of the year because the Detroit dentist and his wife lived there for only a few

months in the winter. A large, white wall shaped like a "U," with the opening facing the ocean, surrounded the house, Barrett said.

Because of the wall, the military had to go back out onto the road. "The motorcycles and Jeeps made a huge racket as they raced to the Sanborns," he said, warning anyone at the house they were coming.

The military discovered the back door at the Sanborns was ajar, and inside Barrett said there were open, empty canned goods on the table. Further inspection showed several people had been sleeping in the beds, he said.

But the most damning evidence Barrett said, was in the living room, which had a large bay window that faced the ocean. In front of it, Barrett said there was a large telescope and a signaling device.

No one was ever caught, but Barrett said the military concluded the people in the house had been signaling to a U-boat offshore to advise them when American ships were passing.

Barrett's sister Martha Barrett Ball, 73, of Dallas, Texas, said during the war, the entire town was required to take turns watching the ocean because it was common knowledge that German U-boats were just off the coast. Along with her mother and brother, she had a shift on Friday afternoons after school from 3 to 5 p.m. at the spotting tower, she said.

One day, when Barrett, then 10, was walking on the beach with her father and brother, she said they heard an explosion as a torpedo hit a boat and saw the fire and smoke in the ocean. "We saw men making their way to shore," she said, adding people were waiting on shore to help them.

They frequently found burned pieces of metal from boats that had been torpedoed, and once found a German sailor's cap lying on the sand. "We took it all for granted, because that's how it was," she said. "There was just no way to locate a sub, and the planes and ships were just sitting ducks until radar was developed."

CHAPTER FOUR

THE LANDING

A U-Boat Commander has the highest status on board his boat. His primary objective is to bring victory and honor to his crew and his boat and to receive the highest recognition from his superiors. In the later part of the war it was a great achievement for him to be victorious and bring his boat and crew back to their home port safe and sound.

During the war U-Boats were given highly secret missions where by they would take unidentified men on board their boat. Their identity would be kept secret as they boarded and even the crew did not know who they were. Only the Kapitan knew but would not reveal their identity until they were a few days out at sea.

The Kapitan announced to the crew that the four men they were carrying were bound for America to perform a very important mission. He continued to explain to his crew that the landing of these men in America would help Germany win the war. It is of the utmost importance that they be delivered safely on the shores of America.

In the mean time these men were snuggled in their little bunks cramped in small quarters within the submarine. They were probably sea sick and scared to death being trapped inside the hull of this U-Boat. Little did they know that they had a long trip ahead of them because the boat traveled underwater all day at a slow speed and traveled on the surfaced at night. Even though the fastest speed was accomplished traveling on the surface it did make for rough seas which made for a real rolling trip for the agents. The U-Boat speed underwater was three knots and on the surface it could do ten knots or more but its surface speed was limited to ten knots to reduce its fuel consumption. As a result it could take as long as one months for a U-Boat to cross the Atlantic.

The Type IXC U-Boat was considered one of the best and it could be refueled at sea by MilchCows which were large U-Boats equipped to supply other boats with fuel, food and supplies including torpedoes.

When a U-Boat had a mission to deliver agents to their enemy's coast the U-Boat was not on a search and destroy mission. In fact they passed up enemy targets so as to not waste time hunting them down. They themselves did not want to be detected.

As they made their way across the Atlantic and in order to relieve their boredom, the Kapitan gave the agents permission to tour the boat, except for the radio room and code room. In most cases the crew members themselves were in tight quarters and manned their positions for most of the trip. There wasn't room to socialize with their neighbor. At night when the boat was on the surface the agents were allowed to go on deck for a breath of fresh air and possibly smoke a cigarette or two. Realizing the importance of this mission the Kapitan tries to make the agents as comfortable as possible so when they arrive at their destination their moral will be at its best.

As the U-Boat approached the shore line, the Kapitan would probably be making arrangements for the agents to go ashore. Preparing the inflatable boat, limited baggage and getting the agents dressed for the landing. Unlike the New York/Florida saboteurs that landed in mid 1942, these agents would not be carrying any boxes of explosives or detonators, only money, cloths and miscellaneous items.

The scene the beach front boardwalk at the Newark Ave. rock Jetty and the Boardwalk Pavilion at Bradley Beach, NJ. The young U-Boat Kapitan would position his boat approximately 50 yards out at sea from the end of the rock jetty. He surfaces his U-Boat exposing only the Conning Tower in order not to create a large silhouette in the evening moon light. There were calm seas that night and with both engines stopped, he watched from the Conning Tower as four German Agents and one of his crew members, dressed in black clothes, inflated a rubber boat alongside his U-boat.

Climbing on board they vigorously rowed their craft towards the rock jetty. It was a short distance to row but for the agents it probably seemed like forever. They weren't cramped in their quarters anymore, finally their mission has begun.

From the boardwalk, people could see the waves hitting the end of the rock jetty creating white caps. Not an unusual sight for this time of the night. Back out at the U-Boat, a crew member will row the agents to shore as a line was attached to his inflatable, the line would help bring him back to the sub as quickly as possible, immediately after the agents have landed on the rock jetty.

The Bradley Beach, New Jersey shoreline was dark, or so it seemed from the sea. Lights that usually shimmered along the shore were blacked out, even the ocean front bungalows had their window shades drawn. The boardwalk pole lights had the ocean side painted black and the boardwalk side showed a normal light. There was also a large wooden wall that was constructed on the boardwalk between the Penny Arcade and the Pavilion to prevent the bright lights from the Arcade being seen out at sea. Bradley Beach was one of the NJ shore towns that took the war seriously. The town and the civilians took every precaution to prevent any light from showing out at sea.

The U-boat was waiting for the return of the inflatable and his crew member. This meant the agents were landed and the Kapitan could soon get underway.

At this time the Kapitan would have told his crew "The darkness hides us as they believe the darkness hides them". But the darkness did not hide the mini signal lights used to communicate from the submarine to the agents in the inflatable. These mini lights were visible from the boardwalk.

My cousin, friends and I were on the boardwalk near Newark Avenue jetty that night when we saw those mini lights and a man dressed in black. Keeping a low profile, the agents ran on the beach from the jetty to the underneath side of the boardwalk pavilion. We looked out past the end of the jetty and saw a blinking light coming from the U-Boat and another light from under the boardwalk pavilion meaning that one agent already made it. Then from the jetty two other men dressed in black emerged, running crouched over. In a matter of seconds all four agents made it to the underneath side of the boardwalk pavilion.

We don't think anyone else saw what was going on because it happened so quickly. Meanwhile the U-Boat Kapitan waited until the agents made it to the boardwalk pavilion to begin their mission. Then using the rope, the crew member would bring the rubber boat back to the sub as quickly as possible.

At this point the Kapitan was anxious to get underway. When all was secure on board, the Kapitan ordered his diesel engines started and all ahead one/quarter to clear the area before being detected. Little did the Kapitan know that he was already detected by us kids on the boardwalk. We were looking at the low silhouette of the subs conning tower as we listened to the subs engines roar as they made their way out to sea. Actually it sounded like a fishing boat which was not an unusual sound from the beach. As the U-Boat began to leave our shores it submerged out of sight.

We realized that we needed to tell someone about this. The first place that came to my mind was the Coast Guard Station located at the Shark River Inlet between Avon and Belmar.

This was a familiar place because it's where my father and family took us fishing on Sunday mornings. The Coast Guard Station was known as the Coast Guard Life Saving Station back then during World War II.

Behind the penny arcade there was a pay phone, so the group of us ran to that location. I picked up the receiver and in those days the operator said "number please" and in a panic mode I told her we had an emergency.

I told the operator I needed to talk to the Coast Guard Station in Avon, NJ. I did get to the duty officer and told him what we saw, the blinking lights out at sea, the man running to the pavilion, the blinking light from the pavilion the whole story. Of course he didn't believe a bunch of kids. "So you are telling me that a bunch of German spies have landed on the shore in Bradley Beach? Kids you know that you can get into a lot of trouble for lying. These are not joking times son, not with a war going on". I told him "I'm telling you the truth, they are hiding under the Pavilion that's on the boardwalk on Newark Avenue and Ocean Ave, you got to come".

It took a lot of talking and a long time to convince them to come. Finally, after we waited a long time, a truck came with six Naval Shore Patrol Sailors armed with rifles that searched the area. They went down on the beach and searched it under the boardwalk Pavilion shouting "Halt, Halt" and they searched down by the rock jetty and found nothing. By the time the Navy got there the German Agents could have changed their cloths, buried their black cloths in the sand and casually walked up on the boardwalk. Four fishermen coming up on the boardwalk taking a coffee break.

Now the agents were ready to blend in with the tourists strolling the boardwalk. When the Navy arrived the Officer in charge told me that the spies may not be here anymore. They

38

had time to walk along with strollers and make their way to Asbury Park where there was a main bus terminal. From there they could have boarded a bus and escape to any city in the country such as New York City, Newark, NJ or even Philadelphia, PA. They could have boarded a train bound for New York City right there in the Bradley Beach railroad station.

In any case they disappeared from history that night and were never seen or heard from again. The success or failure of their mission will never be known.

As a result of my research, I now know that the troops who arrived that night, who came to investigate the incident, were dressed in white uniforms with leggings and armed with rifles. They arrived in an opened end truck which had wooden railing on two sides and a metal tail gate. I couldn't recall the color except it was a medium dark color.

They were from the Naval Shore Patrol Headquarters at the Berkeley Carteret Hotel in Asbury Park, NJ. How do I know? The Coast Guard uniform was Navy Blue during the war years and the Navy wore white.

That's why it took so long for the Navy to get to the Bradley Beach boardwalk. Asbury Park is about three miles north of Bradley. I suspect the Coast Guard Station in Avon did not have the man power to make an investigation; therefore they telephoned the Naval Shore Patrol in the Berkeley Carteret Hotel, Asbury Park.

It took a long forty five minutes to an hour before they got organized and arrived on the scene.

It probably would have been a wise decision for the Shore Patrol to send some men to patrol the boardwalk going south to Bradley Beach. They might have been able to pick out four suspicious characters walking on the boardwalk or they could have patrolled the bus terminal. This is only hind sight and that's what might have been.

Meanwhile back on the U-Boat the Kapitan was glad his agents did not have to go ashore at other coastal resort cities where there were lots of tourist and lights. Beach front cities like Atlantic City, NJ had the boardwalk lit up like a carnival and was filled with tourists. They made no effort to blacken their lights. Atlantic City felt that dimming the lights on the boardwalk would reduce their vacation business. Based on the activity in Bradley Beach dimming the lights on the boardwalk did not affect the tourist business.

Atlantic City kept the boardwalk glowing as did other resort towns along the New Jersey shore. As a result of these lights, the German U-Boats loved to sit off the coast and read the silhouettes of Allied freighters against the city lights. The city lights actually aided the enemy in sinking Allied freighters.

This made it easier to identify the Allied ships before the U-Boats torpedoed them. A sinking was immediately radioed to Sub-Command in Germany and that's how Germany had a record of the subs daily activity. Apparently these resort towns did not get the word about the blackout or maybe the city leaders decided their tourist business was more important than the safety of our merchant ships along our coast. The FBI should have played a more important role to control the boardwalk lighting during war time.

During these landings of German agents in World War II they would dress in black with a cap decorated with the Swastika. In case their landing failed and were captured on the beach they would be taken as prisoners of war and not as spies or saboteurs. Who knows how many spy landings there were on our shores between 1942 thru 1945.

The next day I searched the Asbury Park Press newspaper for any mention of an activity on Bradley Beach the previous night. Much to my disappointment there wasn't any. The agents were never caught because nothing appeared in the newspaper about that night.

We were much surprised that there wasn't any documentation about this landing. It happened because we were eye witnesses to this episode.

Bradley Beach is one of the small seaside towns along the twenty seven mile beach coast of Monmouth County, New Jersey. The boardwalk had concession stands, pavilions and entertainment all overlooking the Atlantic Ocean. Summer vacationers were enjoying their couple of months of hot weather before the kids returned to school.

My family spent the entire summer in Bradley Beach, NJ, since 1939. The first weekend after school closed we were on our way to Bradley Beach and we didn't come back home until Labor Day. Even though we were just kids we knew that there was a war on. We used to find lots of debris washing up on to the beach every day that came from Allied freighters sunk off our coast. Many times the life guards had to clear the water of bathers to remove some floating debris that came dangerously close to swimmers.

There were a number of life preservers, floating fruit, damaged fruit crates, torn clothing, oil soaked rags and much more that floated up on the beach.

The worst debris to come ashore were long, thick wooden beams used to secure the ships cargo to the freighters deck. Also oil blobs, better known to swimmers as tar. All this debris came from Allied ships which were sunk by German U-Boats right off our shore. As kids we were not smart enough at the time to write down the name of the ship written on the life preservers. I wish I would have saved some of those life preservers as souvenirs.

Occasionally we would see some Corsairs Gull Wing fighter planes flying about ten miles out at sea. They would dive and fire their guns into the water. No one knew what they were firing at. Maybe target practice or maybe a lone U-Boat on patrol trying to get away. Occasionally we would see a couple of blimps patrolling the water pretty far out to sea. If the blimp spotted a sub they would call for an air attack to try and sink it. The blimp and the fighters probably came from Lakehurst Naval Air Station, NJ. Yes, that's right, the same Naval Air Station that became famous when the German Blimp "Hindenburg" exploded upon making its final approach to land at Lakehurst just a few years earlier.

That's why we saw those Corsair fighters out there lots of times. So, everyday during the summer we had some interesting times on the beach. We would walk up and down the beach for long distances wondering what we were going to find washed up on the sand. We never knew what we would find drifting up on the beach. Everyday the life guards would spend much of their time keeping the water clear of floating debris in order not to injure bathers.

At night we had our freedom to roam the boardwalk and frequent the penny arcade. We would also watch the vacationers showing off their fur capes and sport jackets. In those days Saturday night was the biggest night of the week when working husbands were united with their wives for the weekend. My father along with his three brothers did the same each weekend. Everyone loved the summer night strolls down the boardwalk in the moon light. Some people loved to do the "people watching thing" and just sit on the wooden benches relaxing. It was so peaceful the strollers hardly knew there was a war going on even though Bradley Beach did their part for the war effort.

People pulled down the window shades at night and blacking out lights along the beach front. Even cars driving along Ocean Ave. would be riding with their parking lights on to reduce the glow along the beach front.

I suspect that since the German agents were never caught, the Bradley Beach Landing story was erased from the record books by the FBI. This landing activity was kept from civilian personnel to prevent panic among them that the enemy landed on Bradley Beach. Of course at the time I was just a young boy and the war was not my first priority. We just continued on with our daily activity of swimming, lying on the beach, having lunch on the rock jetty etc.

Years later I realized that seeing German spies landing on our soil, during a time of war, was one of the biggest events of my life. Telling the story now is almost like fulfilling that sense of urgency I had at the time it happened. Perhaps its been years of frustration held inside. It took the "Library of Congress, Veterans History Project" to wake me up that I saw something big, our beach being invaded by the enemy.

Since there wasn't any confirmation of this act of landing spies on our shores by the Germans, it inspired me to write this story. The story led me into a massive research program that would take more than six years to complete my puzzle.

Below is the Berkeley Carteret Hotel in Asbury Park, NJ. The hotel was a Naval Hospital and Shore Patrol Headquarters during World War II. The Naval personnel who arrived by truck the night of the "Bradley Beach Landing", came from this Hotel.

The picture below was taken by the author in June 2008.

Any record of the Landing in the Shore Patrol Log books have been removed or never written to prevent mass hysteria among civilian beach goers. Fear would have been a major factor if it was know that the Germans have landed on Bradley Beach.

The author explained to his family what happened that summer night during World War II. The view is looking from the Newark Ave Jetty towards the boardwalk. The Pavilion and the Penny Arcade have since been removed.

The above picture was taken by the author's family in June 2008.

Photo taken from the beach side of the Newark Ave Rock Jetty. The German U-Boat was located about fifty yards off the end of this jetty during the Landing.

From left to right, the author – authors grandson Brendan and son Jeff, who helped with the research for this book.

The above picture was taken by the author's family in June 2008.

The Coast Guard Station at Shark River Inlet as it stands today. During World War II it was known as Coast Guard Life Saving Station.

The above photos were taken by the author in June 2008

Bradley Beach, NJ, in the1940's.

Sketch by Orene Koenig

The Asbury Park Sunday Press – June 28, 1942.

Published every Sunday at 600 Mattison Ave., Asbury Park, N. J.   PRICE FIVE CENTS

Army to Block Use Of Beaches at Night

Hoover Reveals Nazis Land Spies From Subs

Gang Caught With Detailed Plans to Destroy Factories

NEW YORK (AP) — J. Edgar Hoover. director of the Federal Bureau of Investigation. announced last night that the F. B. I. had apprehended eight alien agents who landed along the east coast from two German submarines.

Hoover said that four of the Germans were landed "on Long Island" on June 13 last and that the other four were landed on Jacksonville Beach. Fla.

The eight men are now in custody in New York. Hoover said.

Hoover said that the agents crossed the Atlantic. the two German subs leaving France late last May.

The first submarine. Hoover said, appeared June 13 off Anagansett Beach. L. I., and put ashore four Germans. The U-boat came up about 500 yards from the beach. and the men were landed in a rubber boat.

Hoover said the men changed from their Nazi uniforms to civilian clothes. and then planted loads of T. N. T. and time-clock fuses in the beach. They then split up. and went to New York city, he said.

Hoover declared the second submarine landed four other German agents later in Florida, just south of Sontevra Beach. near Jacksonville. These men also came ashore in a rubber boat. and carried out the

(See SPIES Page 2)

Heavily-Armed Soldiers to Enforce Military 'Request' For Cooperation

Strengthening of armed military beach patrols and a direct appeal to all civilians to remain off beaches during periods of darkness were reported last night at Fort Hancock, headquarters of the harbor defenses of Sandy Hook.

A spokesman for Brig. Gen. Philip S. Gage, commandant, said that while persons would be asked to stay off beaches at night, the request did not apply to boardwalks hotels, and other amusement centers on the water's edge.

Explaining that the appeal should not be construed as an "order," he added that it was an appeal for "public cooperation in the interest of national security." Persons on the beaches, however, were instructed by armed soldiers to get off the beaches.

Lt. Conger Brown, public relations officer at the post, declined to elaborate on the announcement, but added perhaps significantly, that the patrols have been strengthened. That has been evident to Shore residents for several days. Many have been confronted by heavily-armed sentries, stationed on the beaches. The appeal was made, Brown pointed out, because of difficulty army and coast guard sentries have encountered in challenging night fishermen and others.

It was also disclosed last night that in line with maintaining a closer watch on Shore beachfronts, several military command stations along the coast have been established. One was set up in Highlands police headquarters Friday with an

CHAPTER FIVE

THE SEARCH 2002

The United States Library of Congress in Washington, DC requested that I add the year and month that the "Landing" of German spies on the shore of Bradley Beach, NJ took place. Adding this information will make my story complete. The extensive search begins with my attempt to find an approximate date for this event. I went back in time trying to narrow down the event to some specific year and month. I ruled out 1941 because World War II started in Dec, 1941. I also ruled out 1945 because that was the year the war ended. Therefore, we know that the year was either, 1942, 1943 or 1944.

A research plan had to be prepared and it all started by doing a scan of the libraries in my area to look for clues as to what I should focus on. It looked like the first place to start was the newspapers dating back to the war years. The newspaper we needed to look at was the Asbury Park Press in New Jersey, some twelve hundred miles away. They did not have computer access to their archived files therefore we needed to take a trip to New Jersey to revisit the Bradley Beach Landing area.

It just so happened that we were staying in Toms River, Ocean County, New Jersey for the summer of 2003. We were close to where it all happened and we had access to the Library. The local newspaper was also in the area, the newspaper that would have ran the news clip about the "Landing". With the help of my wife, Virginia, our first step was to go to the Shark

River Coast Guard Station in Avon where it still exists today. We entered the Coast Guard Station and asked for the commanding officer. Little did he know that sixty five years ago his office was involved in a major search for four German spies.

I briefly told him the story and he was amazed that this "Landing" really happened during World War II right in his backyard. Back then his station was known as The Coast Guard Life Saving Station. The first thing we asked to see was the Stations log books for the summer months of 1942, 1943 and 1944 and if they were available to the public.

Our first disappointment came when the Commanding Officer of the Coast Guard Station told us that these books are not stored here because they are too old. The log books are now stored in the National Archives in Washington, DC.

As noted earlier we confirmed that no landings took place on American soil by Germen spies after the capture of the New York and the Florida group in mid 1942. This was a result by Admiral Doenitz suspending any spy landings to America for the remainder of 1942. As a result, 1942 was not expected to be the year of the Bradley Beach Landing.

Although we asked for the log books for the summer months of 1942, as well as 1943, 1944, we did not discover until later in our research that 1942 was not the year of the Bradley Beach Landing.

Since I was living in South Florida at the time, it became necessary to schedule a trip to Washington, DC for this very important research. Fortunately my older son Jeff lived in Maryland in the suburbs of DC at the time and he would later help us out with our research at the National Archives. Even if it were only to point my nose in the right direction. You can't just walk into these government buildings, there is a procedure to follow issued by the office of Home Land Security following the events of 9-11.

I needed to schedule a trip to DC at a later date. In the mean time we started researching at the Ocean County Library. I was told at the Asbury Park Press newspaper that they do not maintain copies of old papers. They told us we would have to go to the Ocean County Library to look at microfilm copies of the news paper. Since we were still in the New Jersey area we decided to go to the Ocean County Library in Toms River where we requested the microfilm for the Asbury Park Press. We requested the microfilm for the summer months for 1942, 1943 and 1944. This Jersey Shore newspaper is still being printed today.

We needed to look at the months of June, July, August and September for the above years, that's a total of almost one hundred and twenty days. My wife Virginia, my sister Mary and I each took a reel and used the three viewers that were available to us. We spent lots of time during the summer of 2003 spinning reels thru the microfilm viewers looking for a report of the Bradley Beach "Landing".

We looked for some news worthy item that resembled a beach landing. The search was on. Although we did not find any mention of a New Jersey landing we did find some related stories of eight spies that were captured, four in New York and four in Florida. We found stories about the U-Boat battles of the North Atlantic, Hitler's Afrika Kore under the command of Field Marshal Irwin Rommel and lots of other stories about the war.

One can only look at these viewers for a few hours a day so it was a long grueling effort on our part. We had all three viewers occupied for some hours almost everyday. As a matter of courtesy we occasionally gave up a viewer to others waiting to use it. This type of research was becoming more and more interesting.

We thought for sure that we would find something in the news-paper but there were only lots of local news as well as war news. It was exciting to go back to my youth and read about the events going on around the world at that time. It brought back lots of memories.

Much to our disappointment we didn't find any mention of spy activity on the beach in New Jersey. Its was discouraging that here I am an eye witness to a German spy landing on the beach of NJ and called the Coast Guard to investigate but can't find any documentation that the incident really happened.

The Military and Law Enforcement Agencies had already received strict orders from J. Edgar Hoover, then Director of the FBI, that all information about enemy activity on our shores was to be frozen and not released to anyone until the FBI had time to interrogate the enemy.

It had to do with not putting the general public in a panic mode because the enemy has landed on our shores. If the FBI would have captured these German agents the incident would have been a big news release.

I could just visualize the head lines now, "Four enemy agents land on our shore but were immediately captured by the FBI thanks to local residents who phoned the Coast Guard at Shark River Inlet".

It was time to schedule my trip to Washington, DC where I would continue my research. Our next stop was the National Archives, Pennsylvania Ave. Washington, DC. My son Jeff, who lived in Maryland at the time, joined me for our quest for information. It should be noted that the war diaries at the National Archives were declassified in 1972.

If the spy landing information was documented, it would be here. We registered at the Archives on June 26, 2004 and found out it takes hours to get the original log books for the Shark River Coast Guard Station regarding the war years mentioned. It's a complicated set of rules that if you don't go there at the right time you can easily spend three or four hours just waiting to get the reference books. Security is strict and only a limited amount of your own information is allowed to be taken into the reading room.

Any information you are bringing in needs to be checked at the desk. All paper work, reference material etc are checked on both entering and exiting the reading room. The system is efficient and very well organized. There are also lockers where you can store brief cases and other possessions, which are not allowed in the reading room for the time you are there

Everyone was very anxious to help us especially when they heard the story of the beach landing by German agents and what information we were looking for. They finally called us to the reading room and rolled out a cart with only the 1942 and 1943 log books for the Coast Guard Station, Avon, NJ for June, July, August and September. There was one month activity in each book. Jeff took the year 1942 and I took 1943 and we looked through the books page by page and didn't find any mention of any phone call received about some unusual activity at Bradley Beach that night. We needed to finish the years 1942 and 1943 before they gave us 1944.

It took a couple of days to complete our task, although all was not lost since we did learn what was going on in the area during the war. Now at my older age it all made more sense. When you are young your priorities are different. Found it very interesting.

We did get some helpful information from the employees of the Archives, for instance they clued us in on a website called U-boat.net and U-BoatArchieves.net. I will be using these websites quite extensively later on in my research.

I know now that the military personnel that came to the boardwalk that night of the Landing were not from the Coast Guard Station in Avon but from the Naval Shore Patrol Headquarters at the Berkeley Carteret Hotel in Asbury Park. Apparently the Coast Guard Station in Avon did not have more than a few military personnel on duty at the time. Not nearly enough to make a thorough investigation of the incident.

They therefore turned the phone call over to the Naval Shore Patrol Headquarters at the Berkeley Carteret Hotel.

The Hotel also served as a Naval Hospital. Now we had to review the Log Books for the Berkeley Carteret Hotel. One of the employees at the National Archives directed us to the National Archives in College Park, MD. This archives was easier to get to, it was right off the Capital Beltway and not as much traffic as downtown Washington.

This is where we would find the log books for the Naval Shore Patrol. In July 2005 we went to the National Archives in College Park, MD and repeated the request for log books as we did in the National Archives, Washington, DC. It's the same waiting game to get these over sixty year old log books to us in the reading room. The security here was the basically the same as DC, the procedure is very well organized and efficient.

After reviewing the log books we found nothing that mentioned anything about spies landing on the beach, not even a record of the six Naval Shore Patrol personnel who arrived at Bradley Beach that night to check out the incident. As we noted in an earlier chapter they arrived too late to be effective.

We also got new direction from a Naval Officer to go to the Naval Historical Society, Washington Navy Yard, DC and also the Coast Guard Historical Center, Buzzards Point. These historical centers are located in Washington, DC.

We spoke to two historians and they found the story interesting but no mention of any beach activity in their reference books for the years specified.

It appears at this point that since not a word is mentioned at all these research facilities we visited then these spies were never caught and the incident was turned over to FBI. There it is kept secret deep in classified files along with other classified files of World War II. It appears that this incident was totally erased from history and kept out of log books all together. However, as we continue on, we will find the lost pieces of the puzzle and all the related incidents will come together.

In order to prevent arousing fear among the general public that a German landing took place on the beaches of NJ, it seems the story was scratched from history by the FBI. I found out that the information is still classified and the files are not available to the public.

I made a phone call from the Bradley Beach boardwalk to report our eye witness account of German agents landing on the beach and you can't find a record of this call?? That is totally unusual and during war time!! The FBI is likely to have this information but they are not going to share it with the general public, even after all these years.

I remembered that we were living in the bungalow when the agents landed in Bradley Beach. The final path of research here in the USA was to go to the Monmouth County seat at Freehold, NJ. Here we could find the date that our Bungalow was purchased and it can be determined from here what date the Landing took place.

With the help of the county clerks they directed me to Book # 1941, which has nothing to do with the year. The real estate data revealed that the Bungalow was purchased in October, 1943. So here we are after all these years of research with a very significant find that tells us that we spent our first summer in our newly purchased Bungalow in 1944. This is the year, 1944, that the Landing took place at Bradley Beach, NJ.

By putting together more pieces of the puzzle we may be able to pin point the month. Extensive research took place over the past few years, researching newspapers, going on library visits reading Naval and Coast Guard Log Books at the National Archives, Washington, DC as well as College Park, MD. All this did not reveal any documentation regarding the Bradley Beach Landing. I am convinced that the documentation for this "Landing" lies within the FBI files, which I say again is not available to the public. The puzzle continues until we find another piece.

Thus far all the research has been focused on information that may have been available at sources here in America. The past few years of research only revealed more question marks. Nothing was concrete and written in stone. Having exhausted all these possibilities, at this point, I now directed my research into looking at the German Archives and the possibility of locating the U-Boat that brought the spies to America.

We did not expect any other information about spy landings here in the USA because this information was never documented, not even in Germany.

These spy missions were highly classified and orders were given to U-Boats Kapitan verbally and never written. Not a word is mentioned about spies, agents or saboteurs in German Literacy that I read unless the spies were captured here in the USA. That's when they told all to the FBI. After the war the information we obtained from captured spies was passed on to the German Archives.

CHAPTER SIX

GERMAN ARCHIVES

Having exhausted all the avenues of research in the National Archives in Washington DC, College Park MD, libraries and newspapers and knowing the Bradley Beach Landing took place in the summer of 1944. My last resort is to follow thru to the "German Archives" to see if I could find the German U-Boat that made the Landing.

If I could find the number of this U-Boat, I could get all the information needed on the month of the Landing, how many spies took part in the mission, their mission, etc. Keep in mind that the German Sub-Command kept excellent records.

Except for espionage, all U-Boat activities were radioed back to Sub-Command daily. The result was that Sub-Command had a duplicate log book of the subs activity. Even if the sub was sunk the records were still in Germany. Especially if unusual activities took place like an air attack by the Allies or the sinking of an Allied freighter or naval ship.

I would like to say again, that we keep in mind that the German spy missions were considered highly classified as top secret and there was never any written orders given to the U-Boat Kapitan. Nothing about the mission was ever documented anywhere and all orders about the mission were given verbally. Usually only minutes away before the sub cast off its lines. The reason why we knew about the Long Island, NY, and the

Jacksonville, FL landing is because the saboteurs / spies were captured or surrendered and told the FBI all about their mission. They didn't withhold any information about their mission because they knew they were not prisoners of war but spies. Spies would be tried and if convicted in court, were executed.

When the FBI interrogated these spies, they told all, the U-Boat number, the number of spies that took part in the landing, what was the purpose of their mission and more. One proof of this secrecy is seen in the memoirs of Admiral Karl Doenitz, Commander in Chief of all German U-Boats. The name of the book is, *"Memoirs of Karl Doenitz Ten Years and Twenty Days"* by Grand Admiral Karl Doenitz.

Reading the book, I found absolutely no mention of any spy missions at all in his book, nothing. In his book Doenitz talks about his new U-Boats being built in his ship yards that will win the war for the Third Reich. It was considered a secret weapon, a type of boat that would have a speed of fifteen knots under water and powered by batteries that would be charged even when the sub is underwater. A Schnorchel that would allow the sub to stay under water a long time until it ran out of fuel.

The Incident in June 1942 whereby four German spies were dropped off on Long Island, NY and four in Jacksonville, FL and the fact that all eight were captured annoyed Admiral Doenitz.

This brought Admiral Doenitz to refuse to endanger any of his U-boats to drop off German Spies on the coast of America. This incident was not mentioned in his book, not one word about saboteurs/spies. There were many weather stations set up in the north Atlantic, dropped off by U-Boats, but never mentioned in his book. That's how top secret these spy missions were.

I also read the book "U-Boat Operations of the Second World War", two volumes, written by Kenneth G. Wynn. This book identified every U-Boat built in Germany during WWII, more than 1,100 U-Boats.

This book lists the activities and missions of all these boats as much as was available from Germany. Remember there were U-Boats that were listed as missing or sunk where Sub Command did not know their location or did not hear from them for months. For every U-boat that Germany sent on a mission, their orders were put in the Sub Command logbook, a duplicate of what was in the boat's logbook. These books were updated regularly as the U-boats radioed in their successes as well as failures.

U-boats reported to Sub-Command on a daily basis, providing information on their sinking or damaging of Allied ships, their daily activity, and any encounters with the Allies. The only landings that were noted in the book "U-Boat Operations of the Second World War" were the ones that were documented by the FBI where by all the saboteurs/spies were either captured or gave themselves up. This research has formed itself into a puzzle, but the pieces are coming together.

Fortunately, while we were at the National Archives in College Park, MD, we got a lead from one of the agents that there is a website that lists German U-boats.

The website is:

<u-boatarchive.net>

This website was created and is being administered by Jerry Mason, Ret US Navy. Thanks to Jerry for his help locating books and websites regarding German U-boats.

We started our search by looking for all the U-boats that were operating along the east coast of North America in 1944. Fortunately, at that time there weren't many U-Boats operating in the Atlantic.

Most were operating in the English Channel and the area around Gibraltar. Hitler's war was already being lost in Europe and many of his U-Boats were either damaged or sunk and he also lost his Sub Bases along the French Coast. Things were looking pretty bleak for the Third Reich.

Looking thru the U-boat logbooks, I narrowed our search down to five U-boats, U-289, U-955, U-869, U-1229 and U-1230. These were the only boats that were patrolling the east coast of America. Some were patrolling as far north as Iceland. But they all had a mission.

With the exception of the U-869, all these U-Boats were given missions to land spies on our coast in 1944. After the crew of these boats were captured or surrendered they were interrogated by the FBI and told all about their mission. At this point in the war some German Navy men were no longer devoted to the war, so it was easy for them to give up to the Allies.

It should be noted at this time that the U-Boat crews and officers, under Karl Doenitz, were not members of the Nazi Party. In fact Karl Doenitz insisted that his officers use the hand salute and not the heil Hitler salute.

Here is a brief activity listed for the five U-Boats patrolling the east coast of USA in 1944.

April 25, 1944   U-289 Commanded by Kapitanleutnant Alexander Hellwig dropped off two espionage agents Sverrir Matthiason and Magnus Guobjornsson on Iceland to set up a weather/lookout station. Both agents surrendered at the end of the war.
   • U-289 was commissioned on July 10, 1943.
   • *U-289 did not sink or damage any Allied ships.*
   • U-289 sunk on May 31, 1944; all 51 hands were lost.

April 30, 1944   U-955 Commanded by Oberleutnant Hans Heinrich Baden dropped off three espionage agents, Ernst Fresenius, Sigurour Julisson and Hjalti Bjornsson on Iceland to set up a weather/lookout station. All three agents surrendered at the end of the war.
   • U-955 was commissioned on December 31, 1942
   • *U-955 did not sink or damage any Allied ships,*
   • U-955 sunk on June 7, 1944; all 50 hands were lost.

Note that U-289 and U-955 can be eliminated from possibly doing the Bradley Beach landing because both were sunk before July, 1944.

April 15, 1944 U-869 Commanded by Kapitanleutnant Helmuth Neuerburg was secretly ordered to patrol the East coast of America. His patrol area was approximately 60 miles south of New York City along the New Jersey coast. After completing his mission, U-869 then returned to its sub base and was docked at Stettin, Germany, in August 30, 1944.
- U-869 was commissioned January 26, 1944.
- *U-869 did not sink or damage any Allied ships.*
- U-869 sunk on February 11, 1945; all 56 hands were lost.

August 20, 1944   U-1229 Commanded by Korvettekapitan Arnim Zinke was on a mission to land an espionage agent, Oskar Mantel in the Gulf of Maine; however, before they reached their destination, the U-1229 was sunk. There were 18 dead and 41 survivors.

Oskar Mantel was one of the survivors. Upon capture he told the FBI that Germany was building V2 rocket launchers to be installed on German U-Boats. These boats could cruise right up to our shore and attack the big cities of the USA.

The problem was the U-Boat deck could not withstand the lift-off blast. Germany was working very hard to solve this problem, but a solution was never to be found. Also, it is interesting to note that if Adolph Hitler would have launched his V2 rockets against the seaports of southern England instead of London, D-Day would have been delayed or even cancelled.
- U-1229 was commissioned January 13, 1944.
- *U-1229 did not sink or damage any Allied ships.*
- U-1229 sunk August 20, 1944, 18 dead and 41 survivors.

October 8, 1944   U1230 Commanded by Kapitanleutnant Hans Hilbig departed Horton, Norway on October 8, 1944 for its only patrol. On November 29, 1944 U-1230 landed two German agents on Hancock Point in the Gulf of Maine. The agents were seen, then followed and quickly captured in New York City.

On December 3, 1944, U-1230 resumed its war patrol, she torpedoed and sunk the Canadian steamer, SS Cornwallis. U-1230 returned to Norway on February 13, 1945 and at the end of World War II she surrendered to the Allies.
- U-1230 was commissioned January 26, 1944.
- U-1230 sank one ship, Canadian Steamer, SS Cornwallis.
- U-1230 surrendered at the end of the World War II

At this point we had identified the five boats that were in the Atlantic Ocean off our coast in 1944, the year of the Bradley Beach landing. Located in various areas off our coast they all had a specific mission, spy landing.

Also note that, with the exception of the U-1230, none of these boats sunk or damaged any Allied ships because that was not their mission. Their mission was to drop off German Agents on our coast. In 1944 the Allies had submarine detection equipment that if a U-Boat gave away his location by torpedo-ing a ship, the sub was located and sunk.

Since all these boats carried German agents, their primary mission was to drop these agents on the shores of the USA. With the process of elimination, we have previously eliminated U-289 and U-955 because they were sunk before the summer of 1944, which leaves the U-869, U-1229 and U-1230. The U-1229 was sunk before the agent was landed in Maine. The agent survived and was captured along with other survivors. The U-1230 dropped off two agents in Maine, who were quickly captured in New York City.

That leaves the U-869, the boat that was known as the famous "U-Who" because neither the Allies nor the German Sub Command knew the location of this boat at the end of World War II.

U-869 was on a secret mission and its orders were given verbally, nothing was written. According to German records she was on a training mission in the Gibraltar area. But she never confirmed her location so her position was not known.

Actually U-869 was on her way to the New Jersey coast and the change in her orders to go to Gibraltar was only a diversion for the history books.

In 1991, by accident, a local fishing boat was dragging its net along the bottom of the sea when it caught onto a hulk of steel about 60 miles east of Point Pleasant, NJ. When the word got to shore, two brave professional divers hired a boat and went out to investigate the find. They found the remains of the U-869. However it wasn't until many more dives and several years later that the U-Boat was confirmed as the U-869 by these two divers.

They located a tool box in the U-869's engine room, on the box was engraved U-869. Notice that she never went to Gibraltar but continued on her original course to NJ. She was discovered in approximately 250 feet of water.

By the mere fact that no one, neither the Allies nor German Sub Command, knew the location of the U-869 in 1944 and even right to the end of the war, is an indication that the boat was on a highly secretive mission. A mission that was not documented any where not even in the ships log located in sub command.

In addition she was built without a deck gun; her mission was to not engage with the enemy but to deliver her cargo of spies to the shores of USA. She only had an anti-aircraft gun for protection from attacking allied aircraft. For total secrecy, she was also rigged with a Schnorchel that would allow her to cross the Atlantic without surfacing and without being detected.

She carried a full compliment of torpedoes in event of an encounter with allied ships. But, in order to complete her mission she needed to avoid any contact with the enemy. When found in 250 feet of water she still had all of her torpedoes. The U-869 never fired a shot in order not to give herself away.

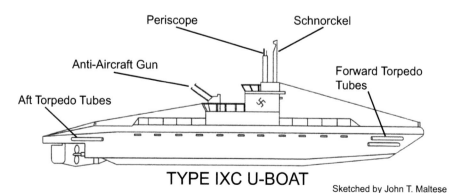

TYPE IXC U-BOAT

Sketched by John T. Maltese

As it turns out the U-869 was the only boat that was in the New Jersey area during the summer of 1944, she was also off the coast of New Jersey on a second mission in December of 1944.

Here is a brief history of the U-869

- **January 26, 1944** – She was commissioned with Kapitanleutnant Hellmut Neuerburg as her commander
- **January 26, 1944** – She was then assigned to Flottille # 4 for training.
- **April 15, 1944** – The U-869 was ordered out to patrol the east coast of the USA within 60 miles southeast of New York City.

This reveals some vital information. Since she was the only boat recorded to be in the Bradley Beach, NJ area in July 1944, then its obviously a fact that the U-869 did indeed drop off four German agents on Bradley Beach, NJ. Beginning of August, 1944 she was ordered back to Germany.

- **August 30, 1944** – She was ordered back to Stettin. Germany and was docked here at the U-Boat Flotilla.
- **December 4, 1944** – the U-869 departed Stettin bound for Kristiansand, Norway where she would receive her new orders.
- **December 8, 1944** – she departed Kristiansand bound for South Iceland where again she would receive new orders for a patrol area.
- **December 29, 1944** – U-869 was ordered to patrol an area off the coast of New Jersey again just south of the

port of New York City. Who knows, perhaps it had verbal orders to make another drop off of German agents.

- **February 1, 1945** – She was sent a message to change course and proceed to the Strait of Gibraltar due to her low fuel supply. On the way to Gibraltar she would meet up with a *"Milch Cow"* in the mid Atlantic. A Milch Cow was a large sub that supplies U-Boats with food, torpedoes, fuel, etc.

  For some unknown reason the U-869 never confirmed receiving this message from Sub-Command therefore continued on her course to the New Jersey coast.

- **February 11, 1945** – U-869, nick named the *"U-Who"* came in contact with two American destroyer escorts, USS Howard D. Crow and the USS Koiner about 60 miles east of Point Pleasant Beach, New Jersey. Both destroyers made a depth charge attack on the U-869 sending her to the bottom of the Atlantic to where she rests today.

On that day, February 11, 1945, the US Coast Guard Destroyer the USS Howard D. Crow was heading southeast from New York City Harbor. Its mission was to escort the Allied convoy CU58. At that time the German Army had suffered major losses in Europe. The Germans lost the Battle for Bastogne, also known as the Battle of the Bulge. The Allies were almost assured a victory in Europe.

At that time the U-869 was patrolling off the coast of New Jersey when she was contacted by sonar from the destroyer Howard D Crow. The Commanding Officer of the Crow ordered preparations to fire depth charges. As the Crow was passing over the sonar contact point she fired her depth charges. The depth chargers would not explode until it hit a hard surface, landing on the sand bottom would not detonate the war head. One did explode with a tremendous blast.

An oil slick was noticeable on the surface of the water. At this point the Crow called for help and the USS Koiner answered the call by changing its heading towards the attack site. When the Koiner arrived its sonar made contact with a stationary object on the oceans bottom.

The Koiner ran an attack by firing more depth charges on the target. This brought up more oil with air bubbles. On February 11, 1945 at approximately 6 pm the U-869 and all of its crew were at their final resting place at the bottom of the Atlantic. Since she had all of her torpedoes it confirms that she never engaged in battle with the Allies.

History never knew what happened to the U-869. German records had her sunk in the Gibraltar area for many years until September 2, 1991 when she was discovered by divers. Location 39.33N, 73.20E.

The final fate of the U-869 was not determined until years after the war. German Sub Command had her recorded as being sunk off of Gibraltar, which she did have orders to patrol that area but never confirmed receiving those orders. She continued to the New Jersey coast.

According to German Sub Command there were no U-Boats patrolling the New Jersey area. She was found on September 2, 1991 and the divers retrieved a tool box from the engine room.

On the tool box was engraved "U-869" confirming that the wreck found was in fact the U-869.

As it remains today, the key information for this entire story is being held in FBI files. These files are still classified and not available to the public. Since the four Bradley Beach spies were never captured, J. Edgar Hoover had any documentation pertaining to this Landing removed from history. He did this to prevent any panic among the civilians that the Germans had landed on our shores.

My phone call to the Shark River Coast Guard Station in Avon, NJ was transferred to the Naval Shore Patrol Head-Quarters in the Berkeley Carteret Hotel in Asbury Park, NJ. The call brought naval personnel armed with rifles and dressed in white uniforms with leggings. Although this episode was erased from Military Log Books, possibly someday the FBI will release the actual documentation for this spy landing.

The crew of the U-869

The U-869
Pictures supplied by the U-Boot-Archiv, Cuxhaven, Germany

Kapitanleutnant Hellmut Neuerburg

U-869 docked in Stettin, Germany during her commissioning
on January 26, 1944.

Picture supplied by the U-Boat-Archiv, Cuxhaven, Germany.

CHAPTER SEVEN

END OF INNOCENCE

Based on the information obtained, we know that the "Bradley Beach Landing" took place on a Saturday night in July 1944. That night on the boardwalk had to be a Saturday night, since that's the night when my father and other working husbands joined with their wives for a stroll on the boardwalk. Men were dressed up in their sports jackets and woman with their fur capes. It was a night to remember with the moon glowing over the ocean, there was even music being played in the pavilion for dancing. There was more entertainment that night than was bargained for. The boardwalk was usually very crowded on Saturday nights.

While all this activity was taking place on the Bradley Beach boardwalk, the U-869 was making her way back home.

It was known that on August 30, 1944 the U-869 was docked in Stettin, Germany. She made her way back safely avoiding contact with Allied ships. The Kapitan knew that coming in contact with the enemy would mean the end of the U-869 and its crew. It could take as long as thirty days for the sub to cross the Atlantic Ocean spending most of the time submerged during the day and surfacing only at night. Cruising underwater a sub could not do more than five knots. Cruising on the surface during day light hours was much too risky.

We also know that the only submarine operating off the New Jersey coast at that time was in fact the U-869. They were on a highly secretive mission with never any written orders given. All orders regarding spy/saboteurs were always verbal. That's why there isn't any documentation of this mission in the U-Boat Command Center in Germany or the German Archives.

Rigged with a Schnorchel, the U-869 was capable of crossing the Atlantic Ocean submerged to prevent her from being detected by allied ships. At this stage of the war an enemy sub that has been detected by allied radar/ sonar, was sunk.

The German U-Boat could not survive on the surface. Allied detection equipment was so far advanced at that time that there was no chance for survival. Once detected, the U-Boat could not escape. In any case, the big question at this time would be why would Adolph Hitler and Karl Doenitz endanger one of their U-Boats and its crew to land four of his agents on the coast of America when Hitler's war was almost lost to the Allies.

The year is 1944; Hitler's Germany is crumbling under the allied bombing turning many of his cities into rubble, such as the city of Stuttgart. Lots of German war material was being manufactured there such as ball bearings used for the Luftwaffe, torpedoes, motor armament and more. The city was being bombed day by day that by the end of the war there wasn't a wall higher than four feet in the entire city.

American B17's & B24's were bombing Germany during the day where the sky was darkened by large numbers of bombers bound for Germany. There were also large numbers of British bombers that bombed Germany at night and that's everyday. Large numbers of enemy military personnel and civilians were being killed or injured and the cities were in ruins.

On June 6, 1944, D-Day, the greatest Allied Naval Armada in World History gathered in the English Channel to invade northern France. Allied troops were now ready to land on French soil to start taking Europe back from the Germans. By mid-1944 Hitler was being defeated on all fronts, the Russian front, Italian front and now France. In1944 there were even several failed attempts on Hitler's life. There were top generals in Germany who felt the war was lost and Hitler should be removed as Dictator of Germany. To continue the war would mean more destruction to German cities and loss of life for the Fatherland. The final attempt was in July, 1944 the same time as the "Bradley Beach Landing", led by Wehrmacht Colonel Claus von Stauffenberg.

In the spring of 1944 Stauffenberg was wounded in North Africa and sent back to Germany. During his time of recovery in the hospital he realized that Hitler must be destroyed to save Germany.

On July 20, 1944 Colonel Stauffenberg attended a meeting with Hitler and his military staff at the Wolf's Lair. The Colonel left his bomb filled briefcase under the conference table next to Adolph Hitler. With the bomb armed the Colonel left the conference room and made it to his getaway car for his trip to the airport.

While he was in transit the bomb exploded and the Colonel assumed that the Fuhrer was dead. He made his way back to Berlin only to find out that Hitler survived the blast and was still alive.

Colonel Stauffenberg and his other high ranking officers were accused of the attempted assignation and they were arrested by the Gestapo. After a short trial they were found guilty and executed by firing squad. Some of the lower involved officers were sent to concentration camps. This was a gloomy situation for the Third Reich and the German Nazi Party.

What does Adolph Hitler tell his armies and generals? What does he tell his people? Morale in Germany was at its lowest and Hitler needed to improve that situation.

Hitler's army was losing faith in the Third Reich, which was supposed to last a thousand years. In light of this situation, Hitler told his people and his armies that Germany would soon have secret weapons that would bring victory to Germany. He was in fact working on several secret weapons. One project was to launch V2 rockets from the deck of his U-Boats. This would allow U-Boats to surface off the coast of American and rocket bomb cities such as Boston, New York City, Washington DC, etc.

This project failed because the U-Boats deck could not withstand the force of rocket launch. The project was still in process to solve the rocket blast on the deck. As for his other secret weapons it was the development of the Atomic Bomb and jet powered aircraft needed to bring down allied bombers. He needed to slow down the bombing and destruction of his cities. These projects were well underway in Germany but needed to be completed as quickly as possible.

This brings us to the purpose of the "Bradley Beach Landing". Aboard the U-boat were four German agents who were trained at the famous espionage school at Quentz Lake outside of Berlin. Their one purpose and one purpose only was to spy on our Manhattan Project's, atomic bomb and jet propelled aircraft and report the progress back to Germany. To save his country from total destruction Hitler needed to know how far advanced the USA was on these projects and how soon they would be completed. Unfortunately these agents were never captured therefore the success or failure of their mission will never be known.

Adolph Hitler did unleash his jet powered fighter planes, ME163 Komet, against Allied bombers near the end of WW II without success or victory. What he really needed was to have the capability of launching a V2 rocket with a nuclear war head from his U-Boats. This would have given Hitler the capability to give the USA a full force attack against our cities and go on to win the war.

Thank God Adolph Hitler never finished the A-Bomb before the USA or life here in United States of America would have been very different today.

THE END

SUMMARY

There's a fountain of information out there. It's just a matter of getting to the right place or places until you find another piece of the puzzle. Find the pieces that go together as they fit into place. Sometimes it gets disappointing when you run into a dead-end. You can't get discouraged. You know the event. You know what you saw and you lived with it for over sixty years, almost a life time. There's no one left to interview, either the players have been forgotten or they passed and there are some that remain unknown. The Bradley Beach Landing was real, it happened on that one summer night in 1944.

As I finished putting all the events together in this book it was like this; The U-869 under the command of Hellmut Neuerburg boarded his boat along with his crew at the end January 1944. He was assigned to Flottille # 4 for training, spent the next three months on a training mission and a shake down cruise with his crew. In April, 1944 it seems he was ordered on a highly secret mission to deliver four German agents to the coast of America. There wasn't any record or documentation of this mission only verbal orders given to the Kapitan just before casting off.

Arriving at his destination in July, 1944 the Kapitan positioned his boat approximately fifty yards from the end of the rock jetty in Bradley Beach, NJ. The agents boarded their rubber boat and made their way to the jetty. One at a time the agents made it to the underneath side of the boardwalk pavilion. The enemy was spotted by four young boys hanging out on the boardwalk who called the local Coast Guard Station at the Shark River Inlet, Avon, NJ. By the time the military arrived the agents had made their way to the boardwalk and blended in with the evening strollers.

The FBI was informed and since there wasn't anyone captured J. Edgar Hoover had the event erased from the Coast Guard Log and the Naval Log. There isn't any documentation anywhere that this landing took place except the eyewitness of the young boys.

The U869 was ordered back to Germany and was docked at its home port on August, 1944. She departed on her second mission in December, 1944. Her mission was top secret and she was ordered to patrol off New Jersey.

Two US Destroyers made contact with U-869 and ran a depth charge attack. The U-869 was sunk on February 11, 1945 with all hands lost. The remains are located sixty miles east of Point Pleasant, NJ in approximately 250 feet of water.

The spy mission was to get as much information as possible on our "Jet Engine Fighter Plane" and the Manhattan Project "The Atom Bomb". These two projects were connected to Hitler's secret weapons that were going to win the war for Germany. They probably would have if Hitler had finished them on time. Fortunately for the world he was never able to finish these projects.

REFERENCE MATERIAL

The following reference material was used in writing this book

- Library of Congress, Veterans History Project, John T Maltese Collection # AFC/2001/001/2030 as Submitted by the author.

- U-Boat Operations of World War II, 2 volumes by Kenneth Wynn

- Saboteurs of World War II, by Webb Griffin

- U-Boats at War, by Jak P Showell

- Saboteurs-Nazi Raid on America, by Michael Dobbs

- Ten Years and Twenty Days, Memoirs of Admiral Karl Doenitz

- Admiral Karl Doenitz, The Last Fuhrer, Peter Padfield

- Death of the U-Boats, Edwin P Hoyt

- U-Boats Off Shore, When Hitler Struck America By Edwin P Hoyt

- Passport to Treason, by Alan Hynd

- Fire on the Beach, by Theodore Taylor

- Hitler's Spies and Saboteurs, by Charles Wighton and Unter Peis

- Landing on Hostile Shores by Jak P. Showell

- The Spies That Came in From the Sea, by W.A. Swanberg

- U-Boats Under the Swastika, by Jak P. Showell

- Shadow Divers, Finding the U-869, by Robert Kurson

- National Archives, Washington, DC

- National Archives, College Park, MD

- Naval Historical Society, Navy Yard, Washington, DC

- Coast Guard Archives, Navy Yard, Washington, DC

- Bradley Beach Historical Society, Bradley Beach, NJ

- Library- Ocean County, NJ

- Library- Asbury Park, NJ

- Library- Pines System, GA

- New Jersey Historical Society, Newark, NJ

- Library- Gwinnett County, GA

- Asbury Park Press News paper, NJ

- Sun Sentinel Newspaper, FL

- U-Boat Archives and Museum, Cuxhaven, Germany

ABOUT THE AUTHOR

JOHN T. MALTESE

Born January 2, 1932 in Ridgefield Park, NJ. Then lived in Garfield, NJ where he attended Garfield Schools and graduated from Lincoln High School in 1950. Moved to Saddle Brook, NJ, to Dania Beach, FL. Spent 29 years living in South Florida before moving to Hoschton, Georgia where he lives today. In 1939 he began his summer vacations in Bradley Beach, NJ where his parents would rent a single room in a rooming house on Newark Ave. and Ocean Park Ave. in Bradley Beach, NJ. The room provided a refrigerator, single cabinet with dishes, knives, spoons, forks etc. in the main dinning room. His Mom cooked in the community kitchen for the family.

As a kid he spent his days on the beach and nights on the boardwalk. Nothing good can be said about a rainy day at the Jersey Shore. That made for an afternoon in the movies and pizza after the movie.

There was a boardwalk/ pavilion and a penny arcade. There was also a bowling alley on the corner of Ocean Ave and Newark Ave where he used to set-up pins for 10 cents a game. Plus he and his cousins did an occasional walk to Asbury Park for amusements and movies. Asbury Park was close by and all this activity kept us busy for the entire summer. Every Labor Day his family packed it all up and went back home so he can start school the next day. This was typical year after year.

One October his parents along with 2 of his uncles bought a bungalow on Ocean Park Ave. Bradley Beach, NJ. The following summer his cousin, a couple of friends and himself were eyewitnesses to a German U-Boat landing Agents on Bradley Beach. This was his first summer the family spent in the newly acquired bungalow.

The bungalow stayed in the family until 1970 when it was sold. The author has very fond memories of Bradley Beach. Even until today he visits with his family.

He was drafted into the Army during the Korean War and after finishing basic training he was ready to go to Korea. He was pulled from the ranks and the last minute was ordered to report to Camp Kilmer, NJ where He received orders to board a troop ship in Bayonne, NJ to be transported to Europe. What Luck, that was like wining the lottery.

From there he was transported to Europe where he spent his tour of duty in Salzburg, Austria. Also attended non commissioned officers of leadership school in Linz, Austria. The same school that was used to train German S S troops. He received an Honorary Certificate of Completion in the course. He received an honorable discharge in June, 1955. Then attended Farleigh Dickinson University under the GI Bill of Rights, majoring in Mechanical Engineering attending the Rutherford, NJ Campus and the Teaneck, NJ Campus.

Even after his tour of duty, he continued to go to Bradley Beach with his family. He had many memories of the Beach and always thought about the "Landing" that took place there.

After spending 48 years as a mechanical engineer and a computer graphics engineer holding positions as a manager and director, he retired 1998. It wasn't until 2002 that he was inspired to write about the Bradley Beach Landing in response to the Library of Congress calling for World War II stories, as told by the veterans who lived it. This gave him an opportunity to present this story as his contribution to World War II.

JOHN T MALTESE

Staff Sergeant John T. Maltese, 1953

WHAT IF ! ! !

What if: At the end of this story we are in the Twenty First Century we see the author and his cousin sitting on a Boardwalk bench overlooking the Atlantic Ocean and the Newark Ave. Rock Jetty here in Bradley Beach, NJ. The Jetty is the only landmark left from that night in July 1944. The old boardwalk was replaced with brick pavers and the Pavilion was destroyed by a storm and removed along with the Penny Arcade.

There was new sand brought in by the Army Corp of Engineers to make the beach wider. In doing so the beach was made higher.

A large portion of the rock jetty was covered, therefore it is now shorter. When we were kids the jetty was a mountain of rocks that went way out to sea. We used to have lunch on it, fishing from it and even go in between the rocks to collect bait for fishing.

Several yards away four men could be sitting on a boardwalk bench, also overlooking the Ocean and the Rock Jetty reminiscing about that summer night when their submarine surfaced and opened its hatches right off the beach.

Four agents went on deck to find a rubber boat ready for them to go ashore. They rowed hard to get themselves to the end of the jetty where they were dropped off. With signal lights flashing from the U-Boat to the jetty to the under side of the Pavilion, with all these mini lights flashing and a crowd of people on the boardwalk, they are amazed they weren't captured. As they sat looking around the area realizing that the landmarks, like the pavilion, penny arcade and wooden boardwalk are all gone, only the rock jetty remains.

Who knows how many times they could have come back into history and they remembered that night as well.

They made their way to the boardwalk and blended in with the strollers as if they were fisherman and then walked into the future. No one will ever know if they fulfilled their mission. Obviously, the information they were supposed to get and who knows if they tried, did not help Hitler win World War II. But keep in mind it came close to being a totally different ending to World War II.

What If the four German Agents read this story and finally unsuspectingly meet with the author of "Shadows on the Beach" after all these years. The young kid that called the Coast Guard and the spies that got away.

QUICK ORDER FORM

Postal Orders Mail to: J T. Maltese
                6372 Rockpoint Lane
                Hoschton, GA 30548

Telephone: 770-967-4601
email: shadowsonthebeach@hotmail.com

Please send book to:

Name _____

Address_____

City_____State _____Zip_____

Telephone #_____

Include payment = [   ] Check   or   [   ] Money order

Cost of book "Shadows on the Beach" ea. ....$ 13.00

Shipping & Handling via USPS Priority Mail 6.00

                Total Enclosed ...._____

A donation will be made from every book to the "Benedictine School" for children with special needs. The school is located in Ridgely, MD. Web site: www.Benschool.org.

PICTURED HERE ARE THE AUTHOR
AND HIS COUSIN JOHN

Both witnessed the Bradley Beach, NJ landing in July, 1944